LIVING ABOARD A BOAT

How To Decide If It's The Life For You

Mike Miller

TABLE OF CONTENTS

INTRODUCTION

The goal of this book is to help you answer in advance some of the questions you might have about the liveaboard lifestyle. I learned most of the answers myself by expensive and painful trial and error. Even so, it was a lot of fun.

The book is about living aboard, not cruising.

There are plenty of websites and printed literature that will teach you the basics of cruising. There are seminars and courses that will give you hands on instruction. Some of this basic cruising knowledge will serve you well as a liveaboard even if you plan to stay in the marina all the time.

Living aboard a boat was a dream of mine for years. I achieved it two different times in my life for extended periods. In my case, I also wanted to do some cruising so that consideration drove my choice of boats.

The first time was on my CSY33 **"Silverheels".** It was a 33 foot cutter with a deck house that let plenty of light below and had 6 foot 7 inches of headroom. I love a pilot house on a sailboat for that reason; motorsailers usually have them. I am 6 feet 5, so not many sailboats have standing headroom for me.

The second time was on my Island Packet 26 **"AWOL"**. Although it was 7 feet shorter on deck than Silverheels, it was pretty close to having the same waterline length. That and it's beamy width made it almost as roomy below as Silverheels, but with only about 6 foot 2 inches of headroom.

I've also enjoyed living aboard my various boats many other times during long cruises, vacations and on weekends. Boats have also served many times as my office and guest room away from home.

I have a lot of experience around boats and love them, especially sailboats. All of my experience living aboard full-time has been on sailboats berthed in Florida marinas.

It seems to me that much of the art of navigating through life involves balancing thinking and feeling. Too much of either can get in the way of a life well lived. As an engineer I've done a lot of thinking, but have also been lucky in getting in touch with my feelings.

The thinking part says that living on a boat is cramped, confining, damp, expensive and invites a feeling among your colleagues that you are less than stable. This might not be good for business if you are a professional who has to dress up and go to work each day.

I have been accused now and then by coworkers ashore of using diesel fuel for after shave lotion.

The thinking part asks where there are anchorages or marinas that are safe and close to amenities. How much will it cost to maintain your boat? How much will a marina or mooring cost? How about insurance? Financing? And so on. You will probably make a list of the pros and cons of living aboard and assign points. It doesn't matter what you do because the feeling part is going to win.

The feeling part enjoys sitting in the cockpit after a hard day at work unwinding with a cocktail. Your old friend the green heron rides on your stern line bobbing up and down and spearing fish on the down stroke. A mullet jumps up out of the dark water and lands with a splash. A large pelican spots him and crash dives into the water to fill his big beak with a tasty meal.

The breeze kicks up and your boat begins to rock gently in her slip. The halyards all around the marina start clanging against the masts and sound like distant church bells. The rain comes crashing down and you go below to read a book, watch TV or listen to music. The rain beats a tattoo on the roof of the cabin but you are snug and secure and all is well. You can hear the shrimp nibbling on the hull of your boat. It's just you and nature.

There is a sense of freedom that you just can't get living on land. Your mind is limited only by your imagination. If you can figure out how to work at home, or if you win the lottery, you can live anyplace there is water and a place to berth your boat. This includes most of the world.

Living on a boat defies rational analysis. It can be just as expensive or more so than living on land, and it can be real inconvenient. Unless you have a huge yacht you will learn where the best laundromats in town are located. You will get rid of all your furniture and most of your books, knick knacks and art.

You will learn how to cook dozens of varieties of one pot meals. You will learn that every labor saving mechanical and electrical device comes with an energy and maintenance price to pay. You will keep your clothing wardrobe to a minimum.

You will feel it was not a sacrifice, but a logical result of the floating freedom lifestyle you have chosen.

Enjoy yourself on your journey through these web pages, and I hope what you learn will help you make the right decision.

PROS OF LIVING ABOARD

Psychological

This is at the top of my list. There is something about the challenges and rewards of living aboard a boat that enhance your feeling of well being. You are doing something that not everyone does, and is also something that many people are interested in doing.

When things go wrong it's up to you to figure out what to do about it and make it happen. There is no one to pass the buck to, and when you solve a problem it makes you feel very good. It is a boost to your self esteem. You are self sufficient.

The gentle rocking of the boat at night when you are safely in your bunk is a subtle reminder of the distant past when we were happy little babies being rocked to sleep in our cradles. It is a very secure feeling.

Freedom

I lived in one marina where my non-liveaboard neighbor was an avid fisherman. He loved to fish with his buddies, and they always went out after dark and came back well after I had gone to sleep. They were usually well lubricated with beer and very noisy.

Finally I complained to the dockmaster and he made the fishermen move their boat to a non-liveaboard dock. If he hadn't, I would have moved to another marina. In other words, you have a certain amount of freedom to choose your neighbors.

You also have the freedom to live just about anywhere you want - as long as it's on water - and still have all the comforts of your familiar home. And if you have a boat that is seaworthy, you can go somewhere on a cruise any time the mood hits you.

Closeness To Nature

Evolutionists say that we humans all originated in the sea millions of years ago. A boat may be a hole in the water into which you pour money, but it is also a place where you are safely cradled by the sea. It seems to be our natural home.

When you live aboard you become part of nature whether you want to or not. Sea birds will get used to you and perch on your boat or dock lines. Manatees will come nuzzling up to you looking for a snack or a drink. Dolphins will cavort around you and blow at you to get your attention. The shrimp will nibble at the seaweed and barnacles on your hull. Wading birds will ignore you as they go about their feeding work. You become a familiar part of their world.

Sunsets are more spectacular, the moon is nearer and the sky is your ceiling as you sit in your cockpit quietly taking in the ever changing scene around you.

Another thing that happens to most liveaboards is a big change in their biorhythm. In other words, you find yourself going to bed earlier and getting up much earlier. It seems the natural thing to do even if you've spent much of your earlier life as a night owl.

Supportive Community

When you live aboard your boat, you have more in common with your neighbors than if you live on land. First of all, you have all chosen the same lifestyle. That choice is more important than what you do or did for a living or where you are from.

The common joys and problems of owning a boat create a bond that is deep and lasting.

Simplicity

When you live aboard, you by necessity learn to keep your possessions to a bare minimum. Your family and friends will understand if they want to give you a gift something consumable will be greatly appreciated. Any other gift takes up space and usually requires you to get rid of something else.

Your eating habits will quite often improve also, and you will lose weight. And since a boat moves all the time, even if gently in a marina, you will find your muscle tone improving.

Economy

Living aboard can be an inexpensive way to live if you do it right. If you are handy around boats, you will save money by doing your own maintenance and repairs. Your small living space will cost less to heat or cool than even the tiniest apartment or house.

In some cases, your boat may not even have an engine. That removes one of the biggest expenses of maintaining or operating a boat. Some folks are content just to stay in the marina and never go out. If they want to move, they call a tow boat. These folks quite often love houseboats.

Living Off The Grid

Forgive the political implications of what I am about to say, but the cost of living just about everywhere in the world is going to go way up. Our leaders have been buying votes for years by promising things they know can't be delivered. They don't care, because by the time the system is hopelessly screwed up they will be retired and living on their comfortable government pensions.

You and I, on the other hand, will be paying more for food, water, clothing, power, medicine, and health care.....you name it.

Your liveaboard boat can be a little self sufficient island that you can learn how to power economically, move efficiently, store the basics of what you need to survive, and push off if need be and drop the anchor in a quiet cove far from the big city riots and food shortages that may lie in our future.

If the bad stuff never happens, you will still be having a lot of fun.

Romantic Image

When you tell people you live on your boat, many of them will say "Oh, I always wanted to do that."

You immediately become a romantic figure that is doing what they think they always wanted to do.

You have a bit of the same image that the cowboy loner had when he rode into town, vanquished the bad guys and rode off alone into the sunset.

Security

If you pick the right marina, you will feel safer living on your boat than almost anyplace else. Many marinas have locked access gates, security guards and good police protection. Another safeguard is your neighbors. They know who belongs in the marina and who does not. It's like having a full time community watch on duty.

CONS OF LIVING ABOARD

Headroom

This is at the top of my list because I am 6 foot 5 inches tall. I've had only one boat in my life with standing headroom, and that was my CSY33. Most other boats, especially sailboats, are short in that category.

Anyway, whatever your height, it's well to remember what your headroom requirements are when you go shopping for a boat. Make sure you can stand up. Having to walk around crouched over is one of the cons of living aboard.

If you can't, you will be able to adjust to it just like I did but not without a few head bumps now and then.

Hard To Sail

If you live aboard, it is not always easy to be spontaneous and just crank up the boat and head out for a day sail or cruise. You would be amazed at the items below that you need to secure before leaving the dock. If you don't, they will be flying all over the place.

You may also need to take down your sun awning, unplug your shore power, cable tv, phone or whatever else you have as an umbilical to the land.

If being able to go boating on the spur of the moment is important to you, you will have to make sure you think of all this before heading out.

Pet Care

Not so much a problem in most marinas, but if you live on a mooring or at anchor it can be a problem giving your dog a walk a couple of times a day. Dogs make good shipmates if you give them exercise a couple of times a day and a place to do their business.

Some liveaboards think it's cool to be a pirate. They fly a skull and crossbones pennant and like to have a bird perched on their shoulder. One of the cons of living aboard is being next to a noisy liveaboard pirate.

Hauling Stuff

If you live in a marina, you will find it a bit inconvenient to be hauling stuff to your boat like food and water, and hauling stuff back off like garbage. If you have a car, it is usually parked quite a way from your boat.

If you live on a mooring or at anchor, the problem is even worse. You will either have to use your own dinghy or take a water taxi. In either event, you will have plenty of things to carry both ways, and quite often.

Leaks

The worst leaks are the ones that can sink a boat. They come from through hull penetrations, and most of us are very careful to keep our eyes open for these. Keep an ear out for the bilge pump and install a bilge pump alarm. One of my recurring nightmares is waking up in the middle of the night with the boat sinking. It's never happened to me, but I've seen it happen to others.

But the most aggravating leaks are the ones that come into the boat through the deck or portlights and hatches. Nothing can ruin a good night's sleep more effectively than a leak dripping onto your face from the hatch over your bunk. It's like Chinese water torture.

It is very hard to find out where a leak is coming from. It's easy, however, to find where it is making its appearance on the inside - usually right over your face or into your radio.

Tracing it to its outside source is far more difficult.

Limited Space

If you find that your boat has just enough space for you, the situation will be greatly worsened if you have a shipmate living aboard with you.

Stowage is always a problem on a liveaboard boat.

You need room for clothes, food, books, music equipment, appliances, etc. You will have a tiny bathroom. On a boat it is called a head. The tiny bathroom counter will be just big enough to hold your shaving cream, razor, comb, deodorant, tooth brush and tooth paste.

If you are a liveaboard couple, you will have to be very creative about where you put your bathroom stuff.

Bathroom

Most boats, especially sailboats, have inadequate bathrooms. The room itself is usually small with limited counter space. Quite often there is no separate shower compartment; you shower in the bathroom and everything gets wet. You use the toilet and it has a tendency to clog and smell bad. And you have to routinely and often empty the holding tank. This is why if you live in a marina you will appreciate a clean roomy marina restroom. It can be a very real bonus.

Lightning

Thunderstorms are a fact of life in most parts of the country. The lightning that comes with these storms loves to find the highest thing on the water and strike it. If you have the tallest mast in the marina, you might make a tempting target for the god of lightning.

The striking photograph above was taken in Hopewell, Virginia by Rick Kidd and is on the website of National Geographic.

There are techniques for grounding your boat so lightning will theoretically find a safe course from wherever it hits your boat down into the water the boat sits in.

It's a good thing to study up on.

Storms/Hurricanes

Storms are also a fact of life. In Florida and the other coastal states in eastern and southern America, hurricanes are a strong possibility each season from roughly June through December.

The photo below was taken from a liveaboard boat at Burnt Store Marina near Punta Gorda, Florida during the early stages of Hurricane Charlie in 2004. The owner may have had one beer too many that affected his judgment. Most liveaboards headed for the hills.

In your cozy home on land, you can either ride it out or evacuate after nailing some plywood on your windows and storing fly away stuff inside. When you live on a boat, you will have no such luck. You have to secure your boat best you can in the marina or move to a safer mooring. You'll want to take your valuables like jewelry or money with you and get the hell away from wherever the hurricane decides to hit. You don't know what you will come back to.

It's also not easy to decide when you need to leave your boat. For example, in September 1992 I was aboard my sailboat in St. Augustine. Hurricane Andrew was forming in the Caribbean and landfall was expected on the Florida coast somewhere between Jacksonville and Miami. I had to decide whether to stay in St. Augustine or head back to my home port in Melbourne.

When you are moving a sailboat, you are moving slow. I decided to secure my boat at a safe marina in Daytona Beach and go home to Melbourne to get my house ready for the storm.

As we all know now, Andrew slammed into the area of Miami-Dade County south of Miami and was a disaster. It was a long way from St. Augustine and Daytona, but that is the luxury of hindsight.

Mail Service

This is not a problem if you plan on living in the same marina for a long time. You can use your marina's address. If you plan to move around a bit or stay on a mooring or at anchor, you can use a private mailbox service in whatever town you end up in. Be advised, however, that the private boxes can't forward your mail to you when you move. I prefer a regular U.S. Postal Service mailbox.

Marina Availability

Good liveaboard marinas are not a dime a dozen. The quality of marinas varies widely from downright trashy to extravagantly luxurious. Many marinas do not allow liveaboards, and others only allow a small percentage of the boats to be liveaboards.

Mildew

Mildew is a moldy fact of life on boats. Most boats are poorly insulated and condensation forms on most surfaces. Boats have even been known to have their own inside rainfall systems. It can be managed by swabbing with a clorox/water solution, but it needs to be looked after all the time so it doesn't get out of hand.

Corrosion

Just about everything on a boat wants to rust. You have to be alert to it on a routine basis. Rusting hose clamps on lines attached to through hulls can sink your boat. Corroded electrical terminations can set your boat on fire. Your electronic equipment can corrode if you don't keep it under wraps.

Wet Walking From Car

In some parts of the country, such as Florida, daily heavy rains during the late spring, summer and early fall are a way of life. A walk from your car to the boat or from your boat to the marina restroom can be a drenching experience.

Dinghy Storage

If you live on a mooring or on the hook, you have to find a place to keep your dinghy when you are on shore. It's best to find a safe place where your dinghy is likely to still be when it's time to go on back to the boat.

When you live in a marina, you can either keep your dinghy tied up securely to your boat so it doesn't move around, put it on deck or on davits, or maybe in a marina storage rack if they have one.

Severe Motion

I have lived aboard on two separate times in marinas that had an extreme amount of wave motion. In one case, the waves came from prevailing southeasterly winds that caused huge waves to come rolling into the marina from the nearby ocean inlet. In another marina, boat and ship traffic set up huge waves that crashed into the marina.

In both cases, the motion of my boat was too severe to even sleep. Nothing could be left loose or it would fly around the boat and crack you in the head. It was impossible to live aboard, and I soon realized that I was the only liveaboard in one of those marinas. I moved to another marina.

In the other rough marina, I was lucky that the dockmaster let me move to a calmer slip further away from the wave action.

TYPES OF LIVEABOARD BOATS

People have been known to live aboard almost anything that floats. The allure of life afloat is thousands of years old. These days most people consider the following choices.

Power

Power boats give you a lot of living space. They have a lot of space above the waterline which means good news for headroom and storage space. All of this space is a disadvantage, however, in boat handling because of the windage caused by the tall deck house and hull.

Displacement boats (including sailboats and trawlers) can only go about 1.33 times the square root of their waterline length. This provides decent fuel economy but slower speeds. For example, a displacement hull with a waterline length of 30 feet has a maximum theoretical hull speed of 7.3 knots or about 8.4 miles per hour.

If I won the lottery and could buy the power boat of my dreams, I'd get the comfortable displacement cruiser shown in the photo above loafing along the Intracoastal Waterway in Fort Lauderdale near Bahia Mar.

A planing power boat like the one in the photo above, however, needs a lot of energy to get up on top of the water and flatten out for higher speeds. It will gobble fuel at a horrifying rate. If you plan on spending most of your time in a marina, you might not want to pay for all of that speed potential with its higher operating and maintenance costs.

There are also multihull power boats including quite a few good catamaran designs. These are more economical to run than a monohull power boat of equal length, and can negotiate shallower waters because of their hull design.

The photo above is a PDQ Power Catamaran I spent a
night with at a marina in Stuart, Florida. I have seen
many of these cruising in Florida, and they look like
great liveaboards. It was very windy that night in Stuart
and the PDQ rode very gently at the dock when many
other boats in the marina were pitching around quite a
bit.

Sail

I have loved sailing since my boyhood days and would
live on a sailboat no matter its disadvantages. I just feel
right aboard a sailing vessel. If you like sailboats too,
you have a lot of choices.

Monohull

As the name implies, these boats have a single hull.
They usually have a fairly deep keel or centerboard that
limits the places you can live aboard. You will usually
have to forego shallow marinas or moorings. Space is
also a problem. Sailboats have pointy ends, the forward
one known as the bow, and the sides of the hull are
curved. This presents a problem for headroom and

storage space. The mast also limits you to marinas that are not constrained by low overhead bridges.

The cutter rigged monohull sailboat above was in Pier 66 Marina in Fort Lauderdale when this photo was taken. It would be a comfy and spacious liveaboard. The spacious pilot house with abundant glass means plenty of light below and good headroom.

Multihull

Multihulls include catamarans (two hulls) and trimarans (three hulls). The advantages of these boats are shallow draft, higher speed underway and a lot of liveaboard space. You have almost twice as much space as a monohull.

One of the disadvantages, however, is you will usually have to pay a lot more for a marina slip unless you have a smaller catamaran with a beam of 14 or 15 feet that can fit in some of the larger slips. Larger catamarans like the one in the photo above will usually require two slips in a marina or will have to be tied off at the end of a tee dock.

Trawler

A trawler is a power boat with a displacement hull that is designed for long economical voyages under power at something less than theoretical hull speed. Sometimes the trawler will have a steadying sail to help it withstand rolling motion while underway. Sometimes they also have "flopper stoppers", devices that you lower from booms extending over the sides of the boat down into the water. The stoppers provide resistance to rolling at anchor or on a mooring.

The trawler in the photo above has tremendous room below because of the vertical sides of its hull and the large deckhouse. It might be tough to handle moving around a marina in windy conditions, but would be a comfortable liveaboard, especially in a marina.

Houseboat With Engine

These are usually boats with a flat bottom and a large house that occupies most of the deck. They are usually designed for calmer waters like rivers or some lakes. The photo above is from the Gibson Boat Company website.

You see a lot of houseboats in inland lakes and rivers. They are usually not considered seaworthy enough to take out in the open ocean or one of the Great Lakes. Their flat bottoms make for a very uncomfortable ride, but in calmer conditions they have unsurpassed comfort.

Houseboat Without Engine

These are barge type boats that are designed to be towed wherever they will be located. They quite often don't move for years. They are usually permanent fixtures in some marinas or liveaboard communities. The houseboat in the photo below was at a fish camp on the Dead River in Central Florida near Eustis and Tavares on the Harris Chain of Lakes.

Motor Sailer

A motorsailer is designed to be a better performer under power than the average sailboat of equal length. By the nature of their design, they are usually a bit slower under sail than the average sailboat of equal length. Many motorsailers have a lot more space than a sailboat because of the typically large deckhouse and hull shape.

The motorsailer shown below has a very large deckhouse and a relatively small sailing rig.

It has a tremendous amount of living space below and would be a very comfortable liveaboard.

Note the Bimini Top over the cockpit and the inflatable dinghy on davits. It is all decked out in red ribbons to celebrate Christmas aboard at Burnt Store Marina south of Punta Gorda, Florida.

WHERE TO LIVE ABOARD

Marina

Marinas can be found almost anywhere in the world, but not all of them allow liveaboards. Sometimes government regulations do not permit marina liveaboards. Other times government will limit liveaboards in a marina to a certain percentage of slips.

A good marina is a fine place to live aboard. The one pictured above is Grove Isle Marina in Coconut Grove, Florida.

You will enjoy not only most of the amenities you did ashore, but you will be part of a unique community. I usually feel I have more in common with fellow boaters than any other group I identify with.

The common joys and problems of boat ownership transcend almost any other aspect of your life.

The marinas I've enjoyed the most have clean restrooms, responsible liveaboards, good staffs who care about the marina and a great location that allows you to be a part of the community.

The marina pictured above is in Dania, Florida.

A nice place to park your car and 24 hour security are super nice bonuses that some marinas offer.

Mooring Field

These are areas with permanent moorings. You hook up to a buoy and usually pay the city, county or local marina for the privilege of staying there.

Many areas no longer allow boats to be liveaboards at anchor. They have passed laws that make you live in a mooring field. It seems to be a growing trend as governments everywhere look for more ways to raise money.

Some of the best mooring fields will have water taxis that will take you back and forth to your floating home. They also will have a place ashore where you can store your dinghy, do your laundry, use your computer or just hang out.

The photo above is from the website of the Coconut Grove Sailing Club in Miami, Florida.

The mooring fields have some of the same disadvantages you will read about below if you are a liveaboard swinging on a hook. But they are quite often less than half as expensive as marinas in the same area.

Anchorage

Some people feel that living on the hook is the ultimate freedom. It's certainly cheaper than a mooring field or marina, but there are some disadvantages too. You get what you pay for.

There is the problem of where to land and store your dinghy when you are ashore. You will be making a lot of trips to your boat to haul groceries and water. You will be making a lot of trips to the shore to get rid of garbage and walk your dog. You have to find a place that will take your garbage. And you have to routinely empty your holding tanks and not in the water where you are anchored.

Energy is a problem. You will have to run your engine every day to keep your frig and freezer cold and to charge your batteries. You may need to add solar panels and wind chargers to supplement your onboard energy.

And just finding a spot to live on the anchor is becoming a problem just about anywhere in North America. People who live ashore on the waterfront seem to have a natural antipathy for carefree liveaboards enjoying the same view for a fraction of the cost.

People who live ashore vote, and politicians know it. Liveaboards are usually too disorganized to form a voting bloc, so you see more and more laws against living aboard.

The one thing politicians are good at is counting votes.

Private Home or Condo

There are many neighborhoods on the water that have homes or condominiums with private docks. The problem is that liveaboards are usually prohibited by local zoning laws and/or neighborhood regulations.

There are some exceptions, like the "Isles" area of Fort Lauderdale along Las Olas Boulevard. A couple of neighborhoods are permitted to have liveaboards on the docks behind small condos or houses. But there are not many places like this and you will have a hard time finding anything at a house or condo in most of the areas you are interested in living.

LIVEABOARD EXPENSES

An excellent discussion of liveaboard expenses can be found in **"The Essentials of Living Aboard a Boat"** a book written by Mark Nicholas that is available either in regular or digital format. Mark has developed spread sheets that look at the liveaboard expenses for different scenarios and boats.

There is an extreme variation in some expenses based on where you choose to live aboard. For example, slip fees in south Florida marinas or the Keys can be 10 times higher than fees in some parts of coastal North Carolina.

Another factor in slip fees is Economics 101. When marinas have lots of empty slips, they cut better deals. When they have a waiting list they don't mind raising their slip fees.

In my experience, marina slip fees have been the single largest expense of my liveaboard life.

Anchorage Fees

There is no such thing as a free lunch, and it's getting harder over the years to get a free anchorage too.

Many local governments hate liveaboards and prohibit them from waters within their jurisdiction. Even though the "law of the sea" supposedly prevails, I have had my hull knocked upon by local police all over Florida because I chose to spend the night on the hook during a cruise through their fair city.

There are cruising guides that will lead you to free anchorages, but these quiet spots are getting few and far between. If you can find one that is located where you like it to be and has some nearby shoreside amenities, you will have entered into the most economical way of living aboard.

Mooring Fees

A lot of local governments have come up with a compromise solution to their perceived problem with anchored liveaboards. That is the **mooring field**.

Such a zone has dozens or hundreds of permanent moorings where a mooring buoy is secured to a heavy weight resting on the bottom. Many of the mooring systems are designed to withstand storm force winds and seas.

A lot of these mooring fields are first class with water taxi service, free holding tank pump outs, dinghy storage areas and access to restroom and laundry facilities ashore. You can even have pizza delivered to your boat in many of these floating neighborhoods.

Mooring fields usually charge about half of what a nearby marina charges for a slip. It is a good way to cut liveaboard expenses compared to a marina.

Slip Fees

Marinas charge for boat slips on a daily, weekly, monthly or long term basis. Most of them add on a monthly charge for liveaboards, the rationale being that liveaboards use more of the marina facilities and use them more often than the person who just passively stores his boat and uses it now and then.

Some marinas include all utilities in the slip fee; others do not and you have to make separate arrangements for electricity, phone or cable television.

Some marinas have gone condominium, meaning that the management prepared legal documents so that each slip owner owns his own space and a common interest in other marina facilities. It's hard for the casual observer to tell this kind of marina from any other; many of the slip owners put their slips into a rental program managed by the marina staff.

Underwater Expenses

In the case of boats, what you can't see can hurt you. You will either have to plunk in the water every month or so or hire a diver to do it for you. Some of the things that wait to be done below the waterline include these:

Hull Cleaning

Barnacles love to live on your hull. They float around in the water surrounding your boat and wait until your hull gets a little green scum on it then they attach themselves to your hull. They intend to live out their boring lives on the bottom of your boat. You need to scrub off that scum on a regular basis and scrape off the barnacles that showed up since you last did it. You will be amazed at how fast the little boogers can come back.

Zinc Replacement

While you or your diver are down below cleaning the hull, you will want to have your zinc inspected. There is usally at least one zinc collar attached to your propeller shaft. The purpose of this zinc is to sacrifice itself to protect your stainless propeller shaft. The water around your boat, especially salt water, is like a giant battery with galvanic currents and your underwater metal parts are like one of the battery terminals. You want the galvanic current to eat up your zinc and not your shaft.

General Maintenance

We've all heard the expression a thousand times: A boat is a hole in the water into which you pour money. The marine environment is harsh and in southern climates that harshness is made even worse by the relentless sun. Some of the things you will have to consider are listed here:

Cleaning

Some anchorages, moorings and marinas are cleaner than others. In all cases, however, you will fall into a regular pattern of scrubbing down the topsides of your boat and doing a thorough cleaning below in your living quarters. If you live aboard in a marina that has a boatyard or allows do it yourselfers to work on their boats, you will have to clean more often than if you live in a pristine resort marina.

Waxing

Hulls and topsides tend to get oxidized and dull looking, and one solution is to wax and buff the surfaces on a regular basis, maybe once or twice a year.

Brightwork

Nothing is more beautiful on a boat than gleaming varnished cap rails, trim, coamings and any wood surface that can be converted from its natural state into a mirror like finish that is a work of art. The work that goes into this effect is grueling, however, and if it bothers you too much it's smart to go with the natural look. Teak weathers to a dull grey appearance that you will never see in the boat shows but that translates to more leisure time for the boat owner.

Canvas

A liveaboard boat should have a fair amount of canvas to make life aboard more comfortable. A bimini top or awning will shelter the cockpit from sun and rain. Larger canvas awnings can cover much of the boat deck and keep things inside cooler on the hottest summer days. This canvas gets torn and mildewed and needs to be maintained properly. Most liveaboards will have a special sewing kit aboard to handle repairs.

Winches

If you have a sailboat or motorsailer, you will have winches. Winches give you muscle power for raising sails and trimming sheets. They need to be taken apart periodically and greased. It is important not to drop any parts into the water while you are doing this task.

Rigging

Sailboats have standing rigging and running rigging. Both types need to be inspected regularly and maintained or repaired if necessary.

Standing rigging supports the masts on a boat and have turnbuckles that allow the tension to be adjusted. These turnbuckles can corrode or crack and may need to be replaced. The standing rigging also is attached at the base to chain plates, usually made of stainless steel, that can also corrode.

Running rigging are the ropes that raise and control the sails. They also get worn and need to be replaced from time to time.

Engine Maintenance

It would be wonderful to have an engine that never needs attention, but that's not realistic. Some liveaboards have liberated themselves from engines entirely and have simplified their lives. This especially works for liveaboards who rarely if ever leave the marina or mooring. For the rest of us, however, a few basics need to be mentioned.

Change Oil

All engines require oil to keep them lubricated and running properly. Frequency of oil changes varies from engine to engine, but every 100 hours or so of run time is a good average. You can do this yourself or have it done, and you have to find a legal place to get rid of the old oil.

Change Filters

There are oil filters, fuel filters and air filters. For water cooled engines, there are also raw water filters. They should be replaced or cleaned on a regular basis.

Change Zincs

Many marine engines use raw water (the water that the boat floats in) for their cooling system. A zinc is installed in the engine to serve the same sacrificial purpose as the zinc on your propeller shaft. It corrodes so your engine does not. You need to know where the zincs are and keep an eye on them and replace them when they are ready.

Utilities

Marinas have a wide variety of options regarding utilities. You will not have to spend any money on utilities on the hook or on a mooring, but you will have to get your energy needs in other ways. Some of the things that a marina will provide and charge for one way or the other include:

Electric

Most marinas have power pedestals at each slip that provide both 30 amp and 50 amp electrical power. Many marinas require a special adapter for you to plug into their power pedestal called a **pig tail**. It's simply a short power cord with plugs at both ends. You plug one end into the pedestal and plug your shore power cord into the other. You can keep your own pig tail aboard, but you will discover it doesn't work at all marinas.

Cable TV/Phone

Some modern marinas also have cable television and telephone hookups on their power pedestals. You can enjoy the leisure of full television and internet service just like your home ashore. Some marinas also allow you to attach a direct tv satellite dish on pilings or the dock adjacent to your slip. Some lucky boaters have their own satellite television aboard and need no additional help.

Water

That same pedestal will usually have a water faucet you can use. You will learn from the sad experiences of other boaters not to hook this water up directly to your boat's plumbing system. More than one boat has been sunk when the high pressure from a municipal system blows out a boat's plumbing.

It's best and safer to top off your onboard tanks and use the water from them. Another bonus of doing this is that the water in your tanks will taste better because you are constantly replenishing it.

Sewer

When you flush your liveaboard toilet, you have a valve system that allows two outcomes. **First**, you can flush the toilet directly overboard. **Second**, you can divert the toilet flow with a valve to an onboard holding tank. In a marina and most anchorages and mooring fields, the second choice is the only choice. Most marinas have a pump out service. You hook up a hose to your holding tank and the junk is pumped out and hauled away to a legal disposal point.

Some marinas charge extra for this service; some allow you to do it yourself. Many popular boating areas also have pump out barges that will come to your anchored boat and pump out your holding tanks for a fee.

Garbage

We humans generate a lot of garbage. It has to be disposed of ashore. Some mooring fields have garbage pickup service. A well managed marina will have abundant trash cans all over the marina and will pick up garbage on a regular basis. Somebody has to pay for it, and it will be you either by having it included in your slip fee or mooring fee or making other arrangements with somebody ashore.

Don't use any shoreside dumpsters or garbage cans without the owner's permission. Things like that give liveaboard boaters a bad reputation.

DECISION TO LIVE ABOARD

So now you've made the decision to live aboard.

You've had time to examine the rational part of your decision and balance it with the feeling part. You are either ready to live aboard or scrap the whole idea and build a little vine covered cottage in the woods.

Let's assume you will decide to buy your dream boat and give living aboard a try.

Here are the steps I would follow:

1. **Make a checklist** of the things you want to have on your boat. Research boating websites, brokerage services, go to boat shows, etc., and narrow down your choices.

Be honest with yourself. If you are not going to sail around the world or across the Atlantic or Pacific, do you really need a heavy displacement blue water boat? Are you real tall? Do you want standing headroom? Will you be living on a freshwater river somewhere? Will you have a spouse or significant other aboard? Does a sailboat make sense?

If you are not a millionaire, it's wise to remember that the smallest boat you can live on will save you a bundle of money. You will have to decide how small you can go.

Liveaboard wisdom: buy the smallest boat you think you can comfortably live aboard.

If you are like me, you will want a boat seaworthy enough to take on a cruise now and then. If you want one that is designed to cross an ocean, however, you will pay for the extra rugged construction and equipment.

Contact a lender if you will need financing to get their requirements. Some lenders will not make loans on boats older than 20 years.

Contact an insurance company also. Some insurance companies won't insure boats that old either.

You should also be aware that some lenders do not like to make loans on liveaboard boats, and some insurers don't like to write policies on them. You will have to check and line up these people before you buy.

2. **Find a liveaboard marina or mooring** before you buy a boat. Many people have made the mistake of buying the boat first, then discovering they can't find a place to put it. You may have to get on a waiting list at the liveaboard location of your choice.

Find out what the marina insurance requirements are, because that could drive the kind of boat you buy and its age.

3. **Find a good marine surveyor**. If you know a good yacht broker, he can recommend one for you.

You need to remember, however, that some surveyors are tougher and more thorough than others. More than one yacht broker's deal has been killed and commission lost because the marine surveyor discovered all kinds of nasty things about the boat.

That's the surveyor you want.

That may not be the surveyor the yacht broker wants. Don't hire a friend who says he knows a lot about boats. You may end up with a crappy boat and lose a friend.

Hire a surveyor that lenders and insurance companies like. Hire one who's thorough and tells the truth.

4. **Start visiting and looking** at your narrowed down list of boats.

Make sure you try the bunk that you will be sleeping in, especially if you are tall.

Also make sure you can sit on the toilet and not have to put your knees up against your chest.

Spend a long time just sitting in the boat and getting a feel for her. Some boats just feel better than others, and it's hard to explain. A wise owner or his broker will let you spend as much time aboard as you want.

THE LIVEABOARD GALLEY

The galley is what the landlubber refers to as a kitchen.

There are some things you should have in your galley to make your living aboard experience as comfortable as possible.

Stove and Oven

Many liveaboards say the heck with making meals aboard and decide to eat most meals out, especially the evening meal. These people don't really need much of a galley. A minimal set up can be a two or three burner alcohol stove like you would use on a camping trip. They won't be doing any baking, so they don't need an oven either.

Here is what the galley looked like on AWOL, my Island Packet 26MKII. The two burner alcohol stove on the left side of the picture is covered with a cutting board. Notice the small air conditioning unit in the companionway hatch to the left. Also see the small fold up counter extension that you can raise when you need more counter space. I could have put a small microwave on that extension if I'd wanted to.

The sink faucets operated on a system pressurized by an electric pump, but could also be operated using the manual foot pedal pump you see near the bottom of the cabinet.

The more a liveaboard becomes a homebody, however, the more he will want a first class stove and oven combination. Quite often these are gimballed so they will stay level no matter the heeling angle of the boat. They resemble your home kitchen appliance but are smaller. They usually use propane gas for fuel.

Here is a picture of the gimballed stove and oven I had aboard Silverheels, my CSY33. A gimballed appliance is most useful when you are underway. It keeps pots and pans on the stove level so they won't go flying away.

The cold plate refrigerator/freezer equipment and insulated box are below the brass lamp and counter to its right. The tilt-out garbage receptacle is just to the left of the stove and oven. The two drawers below the opening port light are for silverware and cooking tools. The sink faucet uses either a manual foot pump or an electric pump.

Fuel Source

The typical liveaboard will have a stove and oven that uses propane for fuel. Propane tanks are usually stored well aft on a boat and in a vented locker so that if propane leaks from the tank it will dissipate harmlessly over board. Propane tank systems also have safety switches so you can't accidentally gas yourself or blow yourself up.

Stowage

When you start looking for places to store your food, you will find you need to be creative. Many liveaboards find they need to shop frequently to restock their pantry. Vegetables and fruits can be stored in net hammocks in plain sight somewhere in the galley. Stash canned goods wherever they will fit and write down where they are so you can find them when you want them. Don't hide perishables where you might forget them; the unpleasant odor will eventually lead you to their hiding place.

Refrigeration/Freezer

Refrigeration units can be either AC/DC or propane. There are also holding plate systems that depend on running your engine for an hour or so a day. The most reliable of all systems is an ice box. A block of ice or a bag or two of ice cubes in a well insulated ice box will keep stuff cold for a few days without all of the mechanical and electrical disadvantages of more sophisticated systems. If you will be living in a marina and eating out, an icebox will serve you just fine.

Microwave

A microwave oven is a nice little luxury, but you will usually have to have a freezer of some kind to keep your frozen dinners until you nuke them. Even the smallest of these things takes up a lot of counter space, so make sure you really need one. They gobble energy, which is no problem in a marina but can be a nuisance when on a mooring or anchorage.

LIVEABOARD SLEEPING

Size Counts

You will be spending 1/3 of your liveaboard time sleeping, so make sure you have a comfortable berth. Lie down and check it out before you buy the boat. Have your partner or a friend lie down with you.

You want something that is long enough and wide enough that you are not forced into sleeping in the fetal position only. You want liveaboard sleeping to be as comfortable as it was in your home ashore.

Also look for ventilation. Is there a nice big hatch above the berth that you can open on hot nights and attach a wind scoop to? Are there opening side ports that will give you some cross breeze? These are good things to look for even if the boat has air conditioning. If it does have air, where will the air be blowing? On your feet, your face or somewhere else? Check it out.

Mattress Quality

Most boats have foam rubber mattresses that are about 4 inches thick. Thicker is better, of course, and some foam is better than others. Innerspring mattresses are great and so are some air mattresses and memory foam models.

If the mattress on the boat you are buying is miserable, be ready to spend some bucks on a good mattress as soon as you can. They often have to be custom made. Quality liveaboard sleeping time is priceless!

Vee Berth

A vee berth in a sailboat is located forward and is usually not very comfortable unless you are sleeping by yourself. The bow squeezes the berth into a narrow zone at the forward end of the boat. Two people will have a hard time putting their four feet up in that pointy vee. Some people who live aboard alone put their heads up in the pointy vee instead of their feet. Take a real careful look at the vee berth if that's where you plan to sleep.

Here is a picture looking forward into the very roomy vee berth on AWOL, my Island Packet 26 MKII. The blue box in the foreground is where I kept my foldable clothes, socks and underwear. My hanging clothes were on a big hook on the bulkhead just around the corner to starboard.

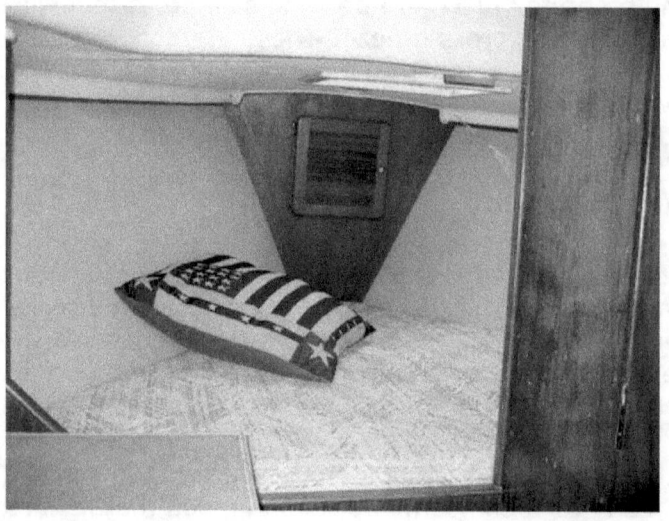

The vee berth in my CSY 33 was not quite as big as the one on the Island Packet, but the stateroom was larger with a couple of hanging lockers and a chest of drawers built in. The notch in the foreground was filled in by the vee shaped cushion with the hat on it. I still have the hat.

I installed a portable air conditioner In the hatch above the bunk which did a good job of keeping the sleeping area super cool during the hot Florida summers.

The sleeping cabin had a door that closed it off from the rest of the boat. You can see the door knob to the left in the photo above.

Pullman Berth

A pullman berth fits along one side of your sleeping quarters and gives you standing room on the other side.

It's also easier to make up than a vee berth, and some of them are large enough to sleep two people.

A good example of the pullman berth is in the Nonsuch 30 Ultra, a cat rigged sailboat. This double pullman berth is tucked away up forward on the port side of the boat. It is long enough for me, and the Nonsuch 30 is one of the boats I am considering when I resume my liveaboard life.

Island Berth

Bigger boats have the space for island berths. These are beds that you can walk completely around on three sides just like your bed at home. They make liveaboard sleeping akin to a luxurious hotel room.

It makes the bed easy to make up, but it takes a lot of space in your sleeping cabin. These island berths are quite often installed in aft cabins where the width of the boat is greater than it is up at the bow.

Quarter Berth

These berths are normally located in either the port or starboard aft quarter of the boat. They usually take up space under the cockpit seats and are a bit like sleeping in a coffin. They are snug and secure, however, and a great place to sleep while underway because it keeps you close to the cockpit.

Most quarter berths get used for storage instead of liveaboard sleeping.

Ventilation

One of the great things about living aboard is getting close to nature. In Florida summers, however, most liveaboards have air conditioning and keep the boat tightly buttoned up from May through October.

Some people have learned to live without air conditioning, and have learned how important it is to have a boat with good ventilation. This means the boat should have plenty of opening hatches and ports, and plenty of low energy draining electric fans.

My CSY 33 had several opening deck hatches and opening ports along with several low drain electric fans. Still, I installed a Cruise n Carry air conditioner on the forward hatch.

LIVEABOARD BOAT SYSTEMS

Your liveaboard boat systems need to be monitored and kept in good working order. If you are very handy, you'll save a lot of money doing the work yourself. If not, you will always be able to find someone around boats who is handy and can help you for a fee.

Here are some of the liveaboard boat systems you might have on your own dream boat:

Heating and Air Conditioning

Boats can have a variety of heating systems. Both of my liveaboard boats had diesel heaters in the main cabin that were piped into the boat's fuel system. Since I lived in Florida, I removed these heaters and sold them at marine flea markets. On those few cold days when I needed heat, I had a portable electric floor heater that I bought at WalMart. It worked fine, and could be stashed away in a locker when not needed.

Some boats have "central" air conditioning with the compressor and air handler tucked away and cold air blown through the boat in ducts. These systems usually use "raw water" to operate and you can identify these boats by the constant stream of water being discharged overboard when their a/c units are on.

On this kind of liveaboard boat system it is important to keep the raw water filter cleaned of debris that it will pick up from the outside water.

One of my liveaboard boats had a Cruise n Carry portable unit clamped down on the forward hatch. It was good enough to keep the forward stateroom cool, but didn't have the cooling power to handle the rest of the boat.

On my other boat I built a wooden insert for my companionway hatch. It was designed to fit a standard window a/c unit that I bought at WalMart for under $100. It worked like a champ and kept the entire boat as cold as I wanted 24 hours a day. My electric bill was usually about $30/month during the hot Florida summer months while living aboard in Fort Lauderdale and Miami. I usually kept the air set at about 80 degrees 24 hours a day.

Ventilation

As discussed earlier, ventilation is important not just for comfort but to keep the air moving and help prevent mold and mildew. Plenty of opening hatches and ports is the key here. You can also add a "chimney" to your hatches. These canvas tubes or chutes can be suspended by a halyard over your open hatch and create an updraft that will help circulate air through your boat. It's great to have great ventilation in Florida; it's better than A/C in the cooler months from December through April.

Electrical

A boat's electrical system is usually a combination of 12 volt direct current systems and 110 volt alternating current for those times when you have access to shore power. If electrical systems go wrong from corrosion or wear and tear or for any other reason, you can be burned to death in a fire or shocked to death.

This is why I strongly recommend that a marine electrician be used for any major work on your boat's system. I feel comfortable using my multimeter to check out circuits and make minor repairs. But where shore power is concerned, I would rather have a licensed electrician install the liveaboard boat systems with the proper circuit breakers, connectors and other safeguards.

Power Source

Batteries

Electrical energy can be stored in batteries, but the batteries need to be charged often to keep them good. An engine alternator will keep them charged when you run the engine. A battery charger operating on 110 volts AC will keep them topped off while you are hooked up to shore power. Unless you have sealed batteries, you also need to check water levels in your cells on a frequent basis.

Shore Power

In a marina I rarely use my battery power and take advantage instead of the shorepower to light the boat interior, operate the air conditioning and provide power for radio, television, computers and other energy hogs.

Solar and Wind

When not in a marina, the situation is entirely different. You can get some energy into your batteries using wind turbines and solar panels, but usually not enough for you to be able to run the batteries through an inverter and get AC power for the same kind of goodies you can enjoy in the marina. Liveaboards on moorings or the hook learn how to be very stingy in their energy use.

Lighting

Many interior lighting systems have gone to LED devices (light emitting diodes) because they give you the most light for the least energy. Liveaboards on the hook still use kerosene lanterns quite often. These boaters also need to have anchor lights at night in accordance with Coast Guard regulations.

Stowage

Most boats use every cubic inch of space for storage. The ingenuity of the designers is amazing. My sailboats had storage lockers beneath each settee and also behind the settee seat backs. They also had shelves on both sides of the vee berth compartment and shelves above the settee seat backs.

My Island Packet sailboat had storage shelves hidden by the dining table when it was put upright into its storage position. My CSY had a dining table that had deep storage lockers in its supporting pedestal that could store your entire liquor cabinet. Both boats had abundant storage in lockers under the vee berth mattress. The more stowage you have, the better. Beware boats that say something like "sleeps 5". More berths mean less stowage. In fact, on most boats the extra berths become storage spaces anyway.

Internet

If you live on a mooring or on the hook, you can get a "hot spot" from your cell phone provider. This enables you to get internet through your cell phone. In a marina, you will find many of them have hot spots you can use for wi fi connectivity, or you can get a cable tv/internet package right to your slip.

Television

A lot of budget minded liveaboards use an old fashioned antenna they hoist up the mast with a halyard. If they are lucky, they can get a few non-cable channels and for them that's enough. Others have boat mounted dishes and pay for a satellite TV service. Marina living is usually pretty much just like home. You can have all the amenities if you are willing to pay for them.

I bought one of the earliest flat screen TV's and used it on both boats. It was very expensive back in those days, and had only a 9 inch screen. I mounted it on a bulkhead in the main cabin. It served me very well on both boats and still serves as an extra TV around the house.

Sound/Music

In my first liveaboard experience, I had a CD player and hundreds of CD's stored aboard. The CD's took a lot of room, but the player itself was about the size of a portable radio.

Technology had advanced by my second liveaboard experience, and I bought an iPod. I "ripped" all of the CD's and stored them in the iPod, and gave the CD's to a friend. I then bought a Bose Wave Radio and played the iPod through the radio. It worked great and saved me a lot of space.

Plumbing

The plumbing system on most boats is fairly simple, but you should know everything about it.

Most boats have a "raw water" system and a fresh water system.

Raw water enters the boat via through hull fittings installed below the waterline. Raw water is used to cool the engine, flush the toilet, wash dirt off the anchor, wash dishes and a number of other things.

Fresh water is used for showering, drinking and cooking. Fresh water comes from your onboard tanks. Raw water comes from whatever water your boat floats in.

Propane

Propane gas is the fuel of choice for many liveaboards because it is cheap, easy to get and contains a lot of energy per pound. Most boaters use it to operate their stove and oven, and that's about it. The tanks should be stored in a separate locker with vent holes so any gas that leaks from the tank will go overboard and not into the bilge where it could explode.

Holding Tanks

These tanks hold sewage and are unfortunately quite often located under the vee berth not far from where your head rests while you are trying to sleep. Books have been written on how to keep these tanks from smelling bad. Some ideas are better than others, but the one I like best is to use the marina restroom as much as you possibly can.

Fuel Tanks

Fuel tanks can be stashed in various places and conduct fuel by gravity or under pressure to the engine. You should pay attention to where these tanks are because if one springs a leak you usually have to remove it and replace it.

Water System

Tanks

Water tanks can also be stashed in various places and pipes conduct the water to the galley sink, bathroom sink and shower. Even if you are using the marina facilities, it's good to keep your tank water moving over. It will make it smell and taste better.

Pumps

Most boats have both manual pumps and electric pumps to get potable water from the tank to the respective faucet. Liveaboards on the hook will use the manual pumps a lot to save drain on their batteries.

Hot Water

Many boats have a hot water heater, usually a small tank tucked away in the engine compartment. These systems usually work by circulating engine exhaust water through a jacket that heats up the potable water. These heaters also work on shore power. Other systems use "flash" water heaters that heat water instantly using 110 volt shore power.

Liveaboards on the hook or a mooring can use a portable flexible water tank that hangs outside during the day and soaks up solar energy to heat water for showers and cooking. Showering in the cockpit works very well if you are lucky enough to have some privacy.

LIVEABOARD BOAT PROPULSION

If you intend to stay in a marina for the rest of your life and not go day sailing or cruising, you might not even need an engine. You can find real good deals on boats without engines. Liveaboard boat propulsion won't be an issue for you.

Lin and Larry Pardey are famous sailors who have sailed around the world many times and just about every place in between. They have never had an engine on their boats, and love the extra storage space it gives them and the peace of mind that comes from not having to worry about an expensive piece of equipment.

If you're like most of us, however, you'd like to be able to take the boat out now and then and get a change of scenery.

Here are some considerations for liveaboard boat propulsion.

Diesel

Diesel engines are heavy, rugged, long lasting and economical. Diesel fuel is less likely to catch fire or explode than gasoline. It is fairly easy for the amateur to learn how to maintain a diesel engine.

As an example of diesel economy, my Island Packet 26 displaced 8,000 pounds and was powered by an 18 horsepower Yanmar diesel engine. Fuel consumption at cruising speed of about 6 mph was 0.4 gallons per hour. That equates to about 15 miles per gallon. That's very cheap for a boat of any kind.

Gasoline

Inboard gas engines still give you the most horsepower per pound and are great for boats that want to go fast. A boat going fast with a gas engine, however, is going to burn a lot of fuel. Gas fumes accumulating in the bilge are a potential explosion hazard that one constantly has to be aware of.

Outboard gas engines are also loaded with power per pound, and have the advantage of being easier to work on than most gas or diesel engines tucked away in a cramped engine compartment. The danger from fire is much less because the engine is automatically well ventilated.

Electric

Electric power for boats is still suffering from the same problem as electric cars: their range is too short. They do have some virtues, however.

To me, the ideal engine for a marina liveaboard would be electric. There are not many boats - yet- powered by electric, but I predict their day is coming. I think an electric motor for liveaboard boat propulsion might be great for the marina or moored liveaboard who does not plan to do a lot of cruising under power.

If you will be living in a marina, an electric motor would get you out of the marina for some sailing or short trips and would be simplicity itself to maintain.

Inboard electric motors can be installed where the old diesel or gas engine was located. They can power the same shaft, and other than a big battery bank and electrical modifications shouldn't be too hard to retrofit.

Many companies have been formed in recent years that do electric motor installations, especially for sailboats.

Outboard electric motors are used just like their gasoline powered brethern.

Batteries take the place of fuel tanks.

LIVEABOARD DINING AND LIVING

Space on all but the largest boats is always at a premium. You will rarely find a liveaboard boat that has a cabin dedicated only to living and one solely for dining. One room usually serves as the liveaboard dining/living room, and this creates part of the charm of living aboard.

Your main cabin will usually be your kitchen, dining room and living room all rolled into one. Talk about cozy; it's kind of like the way the pioneers lived in log cabins in the early days of our country.

The main cabin in my CSY33 not only had all of the above, there was even room for a navigation station that I used as my desk and computer station. Talk about luxury!

One of the ways of creating more room below is to have tables that you can use all the time. You use the table not just for dining, but for homework or as a coffee table.

Here are some examples of boat tables.

Permanent Table

There is some appeal in having a table that is always open and ready for use. My CSY33 had such a table, but it could also be used as a convertible table. Even with both leaves dropped down, it still had a usable surface at all times. It made this space the perfect liveaboard dining/living room.

I chose to usually leave the table folded down in the main cabin. When guests were aboard the table leaves could be extended to create a huge dining room.

In the evening, the fixed base of the table provided support for a slide out platform that converted the adjacent port settee into a double berth.

When both leaves of the table were open, six or seven people could sit around and chat or dine in the best liveaboard dining/living tradition.

Foldaway Table

This is a table that is deployed only when you need it. When you are not using it, the table is out of sight and out of the way. My Island Packet had this kind of table. When you were not using the table, it was hinged and folded up against some shelves on the forward bulkhead of the main cabin.

When you dropped the table down, it could be used either in half size as shown below, or you could fold it over again to stretch over to the port settee. It was easy for four or five people to sit around this table.

Convertible Table

The convertible table is one that can usually be dropped and used as a platform to convert a settee into a double berth.

Cockpit Table

Many liveaboard meals are enjoyed in the cockpit of the boat.

A cockpit table in smaller boats can easily serve all of the diners sitting in the cockpit, but can be removed or folded out of the way when not needed.

LIVEABOARD BATHROOM

If you plan to live in a marina and never move your boat, consider converting your liveaboard bathroom into a closet and use the marina restrooms 100% of the time.

Marine toilets are one of the most aggravating things ever invented by mankind and if you can get along without one, you will be blessed.

If you can't do that, here are some ideas.

The picture above is of AWOL, my Island Packet 26MKII. It is a pretty conventional setup with the manual head, small sink and telephone shower.

It has more stowage than many larger boats.

Toilet

The **standard marine toilet** is operated by a pump handle. When you've finished using the toilet, you pump the waste out of the bowl into a holding tank. The flushing water comes from raw water (overboard), and requires a through hull fitting to supply the toilet. A Y valve can be turned to discharge the waste overboard instead of into the holding tank. Many liveaboard boats in marinas are required to have marina staff install a lock on the Y valve so it can't be discharged overboard.

A **macerator toilet** is similar to the standard marine toilet but has a grinder pump with sharp blades that pulverizes all of the waste before it is discharged. The grinder pump also sends the waste to the holding tank or overboard. In some cases, the macerator toilet can be connected to an **incinerator** that turns the waste into ashes. These installations require a fair amount of space and installation expertise and use a lot of energy.

Another kind of toilet that some people have used successfully is the **composting toilet**.

In this device, the solid and liquid waste are separated and the solid waste is "composted" in a peat medium that can be purchased at any garden store. Once you have used it, you crank a handle that mixes up the stuff and sends it to a composting compartment.

The toilet does not need a through hull for raw water, but it does need a vent for gases created by decomposition. The vent is usually installed with a small fan that can be solar powered or draw very little battery energy.

The waste is removed periodically and can be disposed of at any marina or used in your home garden. The composting toilet is about as "green" as any marine waste disposal system can be.

Some people also swear by the **"porta potti"** kind of toilet shown below.

It's free standing, has no plumbing and all solid and liquid waste is deposited in the base of the toilet. When full, it can be lugged to the marina bathroom and flushed away - if the marina allows it. Other than the old oak bucket, this is the simplest kind of liveaboard toilet.

If you have kids, emptying the Porta Potti is a good chore for them and will teach them first hand one of life's "dirty jobs".

Shower

Only the larger boats have enough room to have a standup separate shower compartment.

Here is a photo of a Nonsuch 30 Ultra sailboat with a separate head and shower. It's an unusual feature for sailboats, but the Nonsuch is very beamy with a catboat rig that puts the mast way forward and allows for a spacious interior.

Power boats are more likely to have this luxury than are sailboats because of the space consideration.

Usually the shower is designed with a portable shower head so that you can either sit on the toilet or above it and direct the shower stream over your body.

Even though some of these arrangements include a shower curtain, you will find the bathroom compartment still gets very wet and has to be dried off as much as your body.

Beware of boats where the shower drains directly into the bilge. After a few showers your bilge will start to smell real bad. Hair, beard stubble and soap scum will plug up your bilge pump. That could sink your boat.

It's best to drain the shower into a separate sump and then pump the sump contents into your waste holding

tank. The photo above is the head on my CSY 33
Silverheels.

Sink

Most liveaboard bathrooms have a sink with both hot
and cold water. The sink counter top is usually okay for
one man with modest toiletry needs like a razor, shaving
cream, deodorant, comb, toothbrush and tooth paste.
Most women need a lot more space than the average
liveaboard boat provides. Men may decide not to shave
and to stop using deodorant and tooth paste. Of course,
that makes the women leave.

Stowage

It's nice to have some dry place to store stuff like toilet
paper or clean towels. Unfortunately, most liveaboard
bathrooms are also showers and dry storage is hard to
accomplish. A big plastic container with a snap seal lid
can be handy in these cases.

Pumps

The toilet itself will have a manual pump or an electric
macerator pump, but you can also get electric models to
replace the manual version. Just remember the energy
cost. The sink and shower will also be served by a single
electrical pump, and the sump will also have a small
pump to get rid of shower water.

LIVEABOARD COMFORT ITEMS

Everybody has a list of liveaboard comfort items that they can't do without. Here are a few of mine.

Bimini Top

A Bimini Top is usually a canvas awning stretched over a frame that shelters the cockpit from the blazing sun while you are underway. The frame gives the awning stiffness so it won't tear or blow away while you are moving at a good clip. It also provides excellent shelter when you are in a marina or on a mooring. In addition to keeping the sun away, it is also useful for keeping you dry when the boat is in a slip or on the mooring during a heavy rain. It adds to the livable space of your boat.

Here is the Bimini Top on AWOL. Notice how the forward area has been enclosed with additional canvas and plastic to turn the Bimini Top into a dodger that helps keep the boat dry. When not underway, I kept the center panel zipped in and the cockpit became a dry back porch where I could sit and enjoy the rain.

Boat Awnings

Boat awnings are usually not designed to be used underway. They can be stretched over the boom of a sailboat, for example, to provide shade on your deck and to deflect the rainfall. Smaller versions can also be stretched over open hatches.

My CSY33 Silverheels had an awning to shelter the cockpit rather than a Bimini Top. It was secured to the boom gallows forward of the companionway hatch and rolled out when needed and was secured to the aft standing rigging, the back stays. In the photo below it's rolled up against the boom gallows. It worked fine both underway and on the hook or in a slip.

Cockpit Cushions

Good weather resistant cockpit cushions will add to your liveaboard comfort. The cockpit becomes your porch and you will sit there more than any other area of the boat.

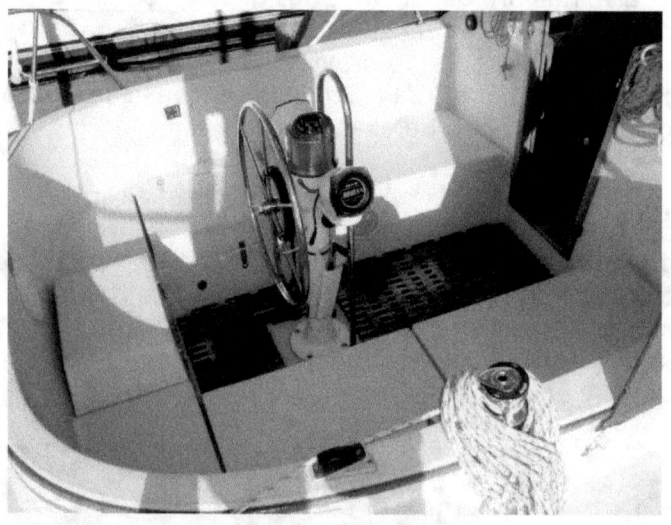

The cockpit above belongs to a Nonsuch 30 sailboat. Good cushions are not cheap, but they are worth every penny.

Gas or Charcoal Grill

One of these clamped on your stern rail will make your cockpit become not just a porch, but a place where you can take many of your meals. They can be fired up using propane or charcoal. Check out your marina, however. Many marinas do not allow grills to be used on boats or docks. These marinas often provide grills ashore for their boaters to use.

Cockpit Table

A good cockpit table can make meals much more convenient and enjoyable. Most of them are designed to be removed or folded so they do not obstruct the cockpit when they are not needed.

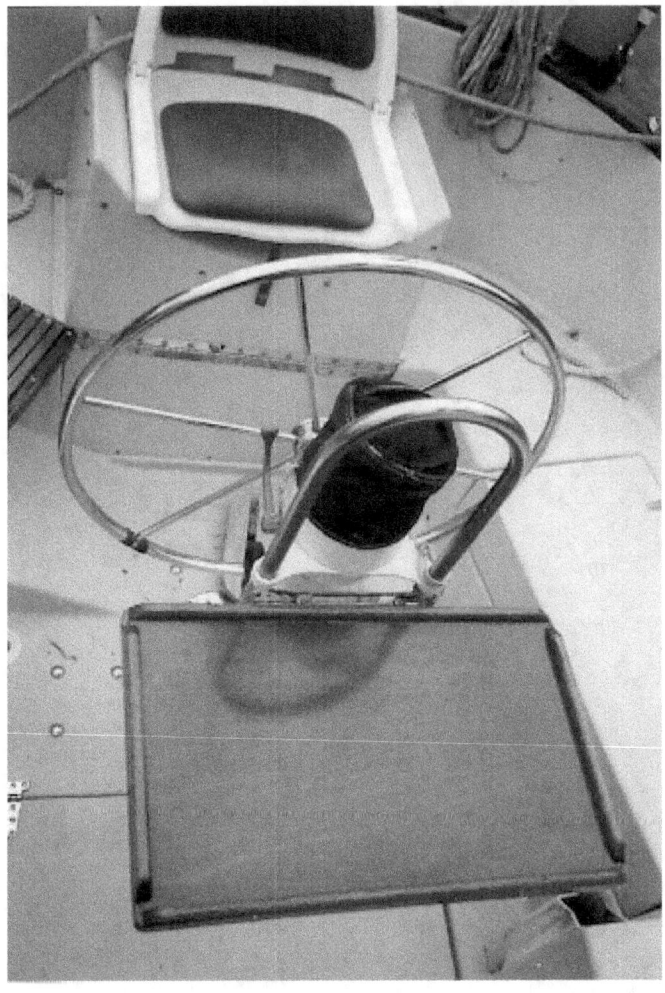

The cockpit table shown above was on my CSY 33, Silverheels. Like many liveaboards, my cockpit became the social center of life on the boat. If you want to socialize with your dock neighbors in the marina, keep your boat in the slip with the stern next to the dock. The cockpit becomes your porch.

If you are not so chatty, put the stern away from the dock and enjoy a quiet place to sit and contemplate the natural world around you.

LIVEABOARD GLOSSARY

If you are a beginning boater, you will discover quite a few nautical terms that don't make any sense to you. This liveaboard glossary may help.

AFT. The direction toward the back end (stern) of the boat.

BEAM. The width of a boat.

BERTH. A bunk or other place to sleep on a boat.

BIMINI. A canvas sun shelter stretched over a frame that provides shade over the cockpit.

BOW. The front of the boat.

DINGHY. A little boat used to get you from your big boat to the shore and back. Rhymes with thingy.

GALLEY. The kitchen of a boat. The person who does most of the cooking is known as a galley slave.

HANGING LOCKER. A closet where you can hang clothes.

HEAD. It generally means the bathroom of a boat, and specifically means the toilet.

KNOT. A measurement of speed. One knot is equal to 1.15 miles per hour. Never say "knots per hour".

LIVEABOARD. Either a boat that is a full time home, or the person that lives on the boat. A cruiser may or may not be a liveaboard. A liveaboard may or may not be a cruiser. It should also be noted that some dive boats allow their customers to live aboard on diving trips. These boats are also called liveaboards, and you will encounter them while Googling for the liveaboard information you really want.

MAIN CABIN. The living room of a boat, also known as a salon and in ancient times as a saloon.

MOORING. A more or less permanent place to secure your boat while afloat on the mooring owner's anchor, as in a mooring field.

ON THE HOOK. To be anchored to your own anchor on your boat. As in "living on the hook".

PEDESTAL. A column in the cockpit of a boat with the steering wheel and engine controls attached. Also a post in a marina on the dock with power, cable, water and other connections.

PORT. The left side of the boat when you are facing the front (bow) of the boat.

PORTLIGHT. A window. Some open, some don't.

RUNNING RIGGING. The ropes that control the raising of sails and adjusting of sails on a sailboat. Ropes that raise and lower sails are called **halyards**. Ropes that control the position of the sails once they are raised are called **sheets**. A sailor that has had too much to drink is three sheets to the wind.

SLIP. A space in a marina where you can store your boat in the water.

STANDING RIGGING. The cables or ropes, usually made of wire, that support the mast or masts of a sailboat.

STARBOARD. The right side of the boat when you are facing the front (bow) of the boat.

STERN. The back of the boat.

WET LOCKER. A closet where you can hang wet clothes like foul weather gear.

RECOMMENDED LIVEABOARD BOOKS

Living aboard can be a lot more comfortable and simple if you are well prepared. Here are some liveaboard books that will help you immensely.

The first two books are complete sources of information about living aboard.

The Complete Live-Aboard Book, by Katy Burke

This classic about living aboard was published in 1982 but is still a very useful and thorough guide to living aboard. Katy is a naval architect and her then significant other, Bruce Bingham, illustrated the book. Bruce is the designer of the Flicka, a 20 foot cruising sailboat with deceptive room below.

Bruce and Katy cruised and lived aboard Sabrina, a Flicka 20, for a long time. It was their home and office; they know what they are talking about.

The Essentials of Living Aboard A Boat, by Mark Nicholas

Mark's book came out in 2004 and was republished in 2008. He covers just about anything you could want to know about living aboard. His book also contains spread sheets that really allow you to drill down on liveaboard expenses and get a good handle on what you're getting into.

His information is current and includes a lot of the modern considerations for living aboard that didn't even exist 30 years ago. His book can be obtained from his website or at Amazon.com.

There are many other books that will enrich your liveaboard life. Here are a few of them that I have enjoyed over the years.

Boat Cosmetics Made Simple, by Sherri Board

Most people who love boats and living aboard do not want their liveaboard home to look like a rundown mildewed faded old shack. This little book first published in 1989 will tell you how to improve and maintain your boat's appearance. The book has been updated at least once, but the original is great too.

Boatkeeper, Motor Boating and Sailing Magazine, edited by Bernard Gladstone and Tom Bottomley.

This book consists of advice on keeping your boat shipshape from the columns of Motor Boating & Sailing Magazine. It's subtitle is *The Boatowner's Guide to Maintenance, Repair and Improvement.* The book is a classic that contains all kinds of timeless advice on boats and their systems.

Chapman Piloting Seamanship and Small Boat Handling, by Charles F. Champman, Elbert S. Maloney and many others including current editor Charles B. Husick.

This is a classic. My own copy is the 59th edition copyrighted in 1989. It is an expensive book, and is continually updated. I think the most recent edition is 2009. It will tell you all about navigation rules, how to read charts, boating laws and regulations, anchoring, seamanship, weather and tides and currents. It's the closest thing you will ever see to a nautical encyclopedia. If you can only afford one book to keep in your liveaboard library, this is the one.

Dockmanship, by David Owen Bell

This small book came out in 1992 and will teach you what you need to know to handle your boat around docks in all kinds of wind and tide conditions. Even if you plan to live aboard in a marina and not do much cruising, you will find many valuable tips in this book. The illustrations are clear and easy to understand.

Heart of Glass, by Daniel Spurr

This book first came out in 2000, and is a history of fiberglass boats and the men who made them. He goes into great detail about the designers and builders who revolutionized the boat industry in the years following World War Two. If you are going to live aboard your boat this book will help you appreciate the other boats you see during your liveaboard life. You will also understand why some of the best built fiberglass boats are the old ones.

Know Your Boat, by David Kroenke

Published in 2002, this handy book will tell you everything you need to do about your liveaboard boat systems. He covers through hulls, plumbing, engines, electric systems, toilets, rigging and about any thing else you could have on a boat. His illustrations are simple and easy to understand.

The Nature of Boats, by Dave Gerr

This 1992 book is a classic of what Mr. Gerr calls *Insights and Esoterica for the Nautically Obsessed.* He covers a bit of the history of boats and yachts and gives you fundamental information on how boats perform in the water and the types of boats that are best suited for specific conditions. Mr. Gerr is a naval architect and gives you valuable insights on picking propeller size, proper galvanic corrosion protection and sail design.

Sailboat Hull & Deck Repair, by Don Casey

This 1996 book picks up and expands on elements of Casey's earlier books. He has some especially good advice on techniques on tracing and repairing those pesky leaks that can make a liveaboard's life miserable.

This Old Boat, by Don Casey

The subtitle of this book, which was first published in 1991, is subtitled *Turn a rundown fiberglass boat into a first-class yacht on a shoestring budget.* Mr. Casey's book delivers on this promise and he gives you timeless information on how to perform many tasks yourself on your fiberglass boat.

LIVEABOARD LINKS

The internet is a constantly expanding universe of information about living aboard a boat. Here are a few links among thousands that you will enjoy.

BOATS FOR SALE

MarneSource.com

YachtWorld.com

MARINAS

Marinas.com

ABOUT THE AUTHOR

I started sailing as a twelve year old on Green Bay, the western arm of Lake Michigan where my home town of Menominee is located. My first boat was a **Snipe**, the next one a **Lightning**.

Living aboard was not really my dream back then because the bay was frozen solid usually from December through most of April. I had not yet learned about warmer climates.

My first experience with living aboard was as a sailor on the destroyer **USS Myles C. Fox**. I loved sea duty and got to see quite a bit of the world.

When I moved to Florida as a young man, sailing became a big part of my life. You can sail 12 months of the year and I did. After many years, I became a guaranteed annual income for my dermatologist because of all the sun damage.

I began to want to live aboard, but with a family I was content to spend weekends and vacations on my boats.

Hurricane Andrew devastated the areas south of Miami in 1992, and I was transferred there two weeks later by my company and worked on the rebuilding effort. There was a huge housing shortage, and the company paid me to live aboard my CSY33, **Silverheels**. I lived at several south Florida marinas.

After that I sold **Silverheels** and moved to Melbourne, Florida and lived ashore for a time. In 2002, my job took me back to South Florida and I lived aboard on my Island Packet 26MKII, **AWOL,** at various marinas in Fort Lauderdale, Hollywood, Miami and Miami Beach. **AWOL** and I finally ended up at Burnt Store Marina south of Punta Gorda, Florida, where I sold her. For now, I've swallowed the anchor and am living in Mount Dora, Florida.

If you enjoyed this little book and purchased it on Amazon, I'd appreciate a review. I read each review and they help me do better next time.

www.ingramcontent.com/pod-product-compliance
Lightning Source LLC
Chambersburg PA
CBHW062015280526
45787CB00005B/2108